Melchior's

By

Patrick Mitchell

Contents

Chapter 1- Melchior Remembers

The golden orb of the sun was beginning to set in the western skies as Melchior came out onto the terrace overlooking his garden. The heady scents of flowers, herbs and fruits gave an intoxicating mix of perfumes distilled from the heat of the day, but now diffused by a welcome cool breeze coming off the sea. The laughter and happy shouts of his grandchildren playing in the extensive garden below never ceased to give him pleasure and delight.

As a royal prince he had received a good education and read extensively, particularly the Greek philosophers and Arabian astronomers. He was a clear and logical thinker and cared little for the rituals of religion. He had long concluded that worshipping blocks of stone or wood, no matter how beautifully sculptured by skilled artists, was ridiculous. However, in order to please his royal father, he had paid lip service to the ancestral religion whilst intellectually dismissing its beliefs as mere superstition. Astronomy became his passion and the night skies his pleasures.

Yes, he had had a good and interesting life and was enjoying his old age in peace and comfort. But it had not always been like that and as he sat down at the cedar wood table with a cool glass of wine and fresh figs, he began to recall that extraordinary journey which he made with two friends almost 35 years ago.

Chapter 2 – A New Star Appears

One night in the middle of winter, he noticed a very bright celestial body low in the eastern skies. Perhaps it was a new star or comet but never seen before. It just seemed to arrive from nowhere. Also, it was moving steadily from east to west outshining everything in the clear night skies. He sent messages to his friends who lived in nearby lands, and they confirmed that they had also noted this unusual phenomenon. Melchior was convinced that it was an omen and felt an overpowering psychological compulsion to follow its path. His two friends, Caspar and Balthasar, agreed to accompany him on his journey and thus their life changing experience began.

Chapter 3 – The Journey Begins

They agreed to take just two servants each. So, within a few days of the star's appearance, (they decided to call it a star for ease of reference), the party of nine men and ten camels set off to follow their destiny into unknown lands to the west. After several weeks of travelling by night and resting by day, they arrived in a fertile land called Judea, a colony of the great Roman Emperor, Augustus, but enjoying considerable autonomy under its local king Herod.

The star abruptly ended its movement and seemed to hover in the skies west of the country's major city of Jerusalem.

Chapter 4 – Meeting with King Herod

As royal travellers themselves, they decided that they would approach the king for information he may have about any unusual event in his kingdom. Presumably, his own scientists had seen the star and made extensive enquiries.

Surprisingly, however, Herod knew of no significant event. He welcomed the foreign royal guests with great courtesy and gave them leave to travel through his lands but asked them to let him know what they had discovered before they returned home. This they agreed to do. From the capital city of Jerusalem, they travelled further southwest and calculated that the star was positioned directly above a small town called Bethlehem.

Chapter 5 – Arrival in Bethlehem

On their arrival in the town, nothing unusual struck them at first although it seemed very busy with many people in the narrow streets. They enquired where they may find shelter and some refreshment and were directed to the local inn, but with the proviso that they would be fortunate to get accommodation but would be able to obtain plenty of food and drink.

They saw the inn near the centre of the town and made their way towards it, the wind blowing up the cold dry dust from the sandy road. The innkeeper saw them coming and came out to meet them. 'Not more travellers', he said to himself, but when he saw that these were rich foreign noblemen, his stony face broke out into a warm, insincere smile. 'Welcome, my lords', he said 'What can I do for you?'

Chapter 6 – The Innkeeper's News

Melchior spoke to the innkeeper:

'We are scholars who have travelled far from the east, following a very bright star which we think could be a portent of great change', said Melchior. 'It has stopped over this small town. Perhaps you could tell us if anything unusual has happened here recently'.

'Well,' said the innkeeper, 'I have never done such good business in my life, and that's very unusual! My inn has been full for several weeks, due mainly to the national census which our occupying masters have decreed throughout Judea. But there have also been several other visitors enquiring about a young family temporarily staying in one of my stables, so I have been doing a roaring trade in supplying these extra travellers with food and drink'

'Is there anything unusual about this family?', Melchior enquired.

'Not really', replied the innkeeper. 'I had to put them in the stable because there was no room inside the inn. I was fully booked.

The young woman was heavily pregnant, so I made the stable as comfortable as possible, moving most of the animals to another barn in a distant field, leaving just one old donkey and an injured ox in the stable.'

'Has the woman had her child?'

'Yes. About three weeks ago. She gave birth to a boy. Mother and child are healthy enough according to my wife who helps them out from time to time and keeps an eye on them. I've not bothered with the family. I'm too busy looking after my guests and running my business'.

Chapter 7 – Visit by the Shepherds

'Are you sure there was nothing different about this birth?', Melchior pressed the innkeeper.

'Come to think of it, on the night the child was born, a flock of shepherds came down from the hills asking to see the baby. Now, you know what these shepherds are like. They spend weeks on end all over these extensive valleys and hills, then come into the towns from time to time to stock up on provisions. They see a few pretty girls, have a few jugs of wine in the local inns and then all hell breaks loose. Fighting, swearing, wrecking property, throwing up all over the place; they are a complete pain. In fact, last summer I had to call for help from the king's royal garrison to restore order after a bunch of these drunken shepherds started fighting at my place. I then banned them coming here again. So, when they came into my courtyard in the dead of night asking about the child, I told them to clear off, or else I would call out Herod's guard again. But they were very polite, respectful even; none asked for any drink other than water.

They only wanted to see the child, they said. How they knew that the child had been born puzzled me; we only knew an hour or so before because we heard the baby cry.

'*God told us to come*', they said. 'Well, I could hardly believe my ears. This bunch of hard living, hard-nosed hell raisers never talked about God, usually all they talked about was sheep, women, booze, and their hate for the Romans. So, I relented and let them go to the stable to see the child. When they came out, they looked - well, happy.

They thanked me and apologised for the trouble last summer. They also wished peace and wellbeing to me and my family. Now that was *very* unusual!'

Chapter 8 – The Kings see the Child Jesus

Melchior had listened with great interest to the innkeeper and knew that they had finally arrived at their destination.

'Undoubtedly, this is a special child. Please take us to the stable, innkeeper', asked Melchior.

'This way, my lords. You will find the father who is called Joseph, wary of you to begin with and very protective of his wife, Mary, who is tired and needs to rest after so many visitors'.

'Do not worry, we will not stay too long. We have brought some gifts which will help to pay for their expenses'.

The three royal scholars knocked on the stable door and spoke gently to the young man who opened it. The innkeeper reassured Joseph who ushered them inside to see the child. He spoke to his wife who smiled at them and picked up the baby from his cot, which was an animal feeding trough full of hay, and cradled him in her lap. She looked beautiful but very tired, her teenage face showing the initial strain of motherhood as well as coping with being an instant local celebrity.

The gifts of gold, frankincense and myrrh were handed to the parents who graciously thanked their important visitors. Melchior, mindful of how he used to play with his own children, went to tickle the baby's chin. As he did so, a tiny hand grasped his finger and waggled it about as if saying *thank you* for the gifts. At that moment, the scholar felt the exhaustion of weeks of hard travel fall away from him. He felt refreshed, calm, filled with an inner peace which he had never before experienced. It was a peace which had stayed with him all his life – a gift far more durable and comforting than the ones they had brought. Mindful of the young family's need for rest and privacy, they soon left.

Chapter 9 – Departure Home

All three princes felt a sense of refreshment and peace which Melchior had experienced. Yet they also felt a sense of foreboding about the Jewish King, Herod, so they decided not to return via Jerusalem to their own countries but went a different route. As the years passed Melchior received periodic reports on the young family's progress from one of his servants who had stayed behind in Bethlehem and married the innkeeper's daughter.

Joseph, Mary and the baby boy moved back to Nazareth where they previously lived. The child's life was indeed remarkable, but that is a story for another day.

We have seen His Star in the East
and have come to worship Him

St. Mathew – Chapter 2

Printed in Great Britain
by Amazon

11097918R00018